now you can join the others

now you can join the others

poems

TAIJE SILVERMAN

Louisiana State University Press   *Baton Rouge*

Published by Louisiana State University Press
lsupress.org

LSU Press Paperback Original

DESIGNER: Mandy McDonald Scallan
TYPEFACE: Minion Pro

Library of Congress Cataloging-in-Publication Data
Names: Silverman, Taije, 1974– author.
Title: Now you can join the others : poems / Taije Silverman.
Description: Baton Rouge : Louisiana State University Press, [2022]
Identifiers: LCCN 2022014613 (print) | LCCN 2022014614 (ebook) | ISBN
    978-0-8071-7853-9 (paperback) | ISBN 978-0-8071-7898-0 (pdf) | ISBN
    978-0-8071-7897-3 (epub)
Subjects: LCGFT: Poetry.
Classification: LCC PS3619.I5525 N69 2022 (print) | LCC PS3619.I5525
    (ebook) | DDC 811/.6—dc23
LC record available at https://lccn.loc.gov/2022014613
LC ebook record available at https://lccn.loc.gov/2022014614

Peace be unto love when it comes, when it dies and changes lovers in hotels. Does it have anything to lose?

—Mahmoud Darwish

contents

III

IV

I

Grief

Let it be seeds.
Let it be the slow tornado of seeds from the oak tree
by the gates to the playground in May wind.
Today is mother's day, and someone said it is almost impossible
to remember something before you know the word for it
and the babies in their mothers' arms
stare at the seeds and they don't know
the word for falling. Nor the words for sudden or whirling.
Let it be something that doesn't last, not the moon.
Let it not be the rooftops that are so quiet.
Let it come to the white doorstep like rain and slide
onto the sidewalk not knowing. What is gentle if not time,
but it's not time that is gentle, what will happen in the future
doesn't matter. Cicadas underground are called nymphs
and their wings look like tree seeds. Trapped under skin
and as soft as the dirt that surrounds them.
Teneral is a word for the days between
when the cicada digs its way out of earth and begins to sing
and when its self and shell are still
a single, susceptible thing. It is impossible
to remember. Let it be the years
underground, molting nymph skin
and moving in the soil without sound.
It's not time that is gentle but what unknown sign,
a method of counting each spring through the roots of a tree.
How they learn from the taste of a root's juice the moment
when in one rush they should push up to earth.
Teneral, meaning not yet hardened, a sense before a memory
of the shell. Let it be the sign in the cells
of the blind safe skin, the limbo of gold
walling here and there, where the baby waits
between a mother's body and the air's tears, he came
to my breast and rested, there was no before.
Let it be the gold room with its lack of door, that time
of day, cicadas will wait until sunset to break through the dirt.

Where did he go while I pushed?
We stood in the tunnel of seeds, windmills, a tree
had come to make promises. Rain to stone, rain to street.
They seemed while they fell to be lifting and we waited, watching,
the baby without words for what we were seeing.
Seeds pushing roots, brick, and dirt don't say
what they know about time. Rise. For days the whole town will sing.

Spiritual Evaluation

IF YOU THINK YOU HAVE BEEN THE VICTIM OF WITCHCRAFT, ENVY, THE EVIL EYE,
OR BAD LUCK, COME INSIDE AND GET A SPIRITUAL EVALUATION.
    —sign on the Church of Jesus Christ in the Lord, Philadelphia

Did you want this baby?
There are a certain number of questions you may pass over
without forfeiting your score on the test.
Do you understand that metaphors involving hummingbirds
are not useful? Do you understand
that you are in no way related to hummingbirds?
If this baby is the size of an a) eraser or b) apricot
or c) memory, will you be able to determine
whether on the day after the hurricane,
the river was as full as a river can be
without flooding the ramp to the bypass?
Heavy rain has been known
to push hummingbirds into bodies of water,
causing them to drown. Hummingbirds
remember each flower they have visited
and on average they visit 1,000 flowers a day.
Define, in one word, your relationship with the unbelievable.
Do you think you have been the victim of witchcraft?
There is a limited number of questions
you may choose not to answer.
Calculate the amount of water in a bathtub
if one eighth of it drains at one half of the speed
at which water now flows down the river.
You have one hour and nine months.
You have six months. You have the evening.
When you hear the word *countdown,*
do you think of the moon? When you picture the moon,
do you see its surface, or a not inhospitable orb
that alternates in size according to proximity with rooftops?
This problem is commonly referred to as *moon illusion.*

This theory is generally known as *shape constancy.*
With the shape of your body please prove
that the moon does not generate its own light. Do you like
charades? If this baby is a girl, what.
If this baby is a boy. Do you think
you have been the victim of bad luck?
Describe in five words what this baby will fear
if this baby is an apricot. List everyone it will love
if it is an eraser. Will this baby's smile be like
a) the furniture in your basement or
b) someone dead whom you loved more than you love
the baby. Explain what it means to love someone more.

Loblolly, Poplar, Sixteen Years

Time has gone out for a walk in the woods
that envelop the house of my childhood.

Are you cold, time? It rubs
against mottled blue scales of bark on the trees.

Bodies in the graveyard have become
a kind of sugar: sweetness of dirt caking stones

that wet ferns have walled in. Death drifts
like clouds across backdrops.

Time in the dark with the rain right now,
gathering hills into misting.

And then, and then, the end, and then.
Patterns of lichen on bark mimic tectonic plates.

But time won't come back to the driveway.
It won't come back to the fragments of slate

we leveled and laid as a path to the porch
from the corridors of boxwoods.

Are you tired, time? A question
for the trellis, for an iris.

Flies, strewn over upstairs sills;
the once-new weeping cherry.

Measurer, fear-caller, wind-meddled gone.
No sign out in front of the house now, nor daylilies.

Ways to Say Luck

The man on the street was a tall peel of bark
and the woman behind him slept face to the wall
of a vacant cathedral, her arm
as a pillow, or the dark as a pillow
that cradled her hair with its dense, knitted scent
of wet heat in the evening's lush air.

So I asked could I bring him back
something to eat, and he answered, *a burger,*
and looked at the street, *And for her too?*
he asked, and he promised to wait when I said
I would bring it back soon. But when I came back
he was arguing with the full moon.

It was bright, and half-shrouded
in white crooked clouds like old washcloths
wrung out, or those end-bits of dreams
you remember days later with no sense
of what they might mean.
I have tried to explain to my students

that we share only symbols, and how
the word *symbol* is also a symbol,
and how any heavily breathing
warm beast is a symbol for a pillow,
or for a version of family,
or for how the soul dwells inside space.

The moon is an old symbol. It follows us
down every block like a dog, and is dumb
as a dog, and as patient, and loyal, and willing.
Tonight when I saw it, I thought of a man
whom I loved once, and how he could see
the same moon, and I hoped if I looked,

he would write to me, telling me *I loved you too,*
then remind me of ways to say luck in other languages.
The moon: a cluster of small broken rocks
that have softened and sealed together in time
or a version of time so long gone and complete
that it can't be conceived in the terms we use

to think. I thought, coming home tonight,
I'm happy. I thought, I am as lucky
as luck gets. I was putting the baby to bed
in his crib, and I'd just bent to kiss
his warm, water-smooth skin when my husband
walked in and I told him, *I couldn't ask*

for a better partner. Every list of what-ifs
and befores, every wall of each school dance's
streamer-draped, windowless gym,
I would choose him. Moon like a dog, moon
that's like no moon at all.
And the man on the street

brought his gaze down to thank me,
his smile surprised, then he raised
his arms high with his palms pressed
and pointed, as if he were trying to mime
the clouds on the moon. He kept nodding to them,
and then nodding to me, to say, *Look. See?*

I wanted to tell the baby about it.
Once, in a story, the moon fell in love
with a sleeping young boy, so she let
the boy choose his own fate while he slept.
Who would hear me, if I told the baby?
What happens in the future is less moon than moon.

When I was a baby, my mother would write to me,
telling me what I was like each new month, and now
sometimes at night, I reread her letters, then fall asleep
dreaming that she's still alive, and I beg her again
every night not to die since it seems in the dreams
she can help it. *You are a delight,* she writes to me.

I dream I can see the whole ocean below me,
239,000 miles down, which is the height of a hill town
we've come with the baby, but I keep getting lost,
all the turns through steep passes have turned
into rooftops of foreign stone houses and is that
new snow or just light on these peaks, am I sleeping?

*Who knows how many moons of distance
separate us by now,* wrote the man I once loved
while I asked for two cheeseburgers, fries
and large sprites, then brought them
to strangers and walked through my longing
to you: breathing baby, freed fate of the future, my family.

The light from the moon is more miles away
than the playground on Spruce with the swing set
constructed for babies. It's the best I can do.
I found my way home toward the end of the dream
and still dreaming I slept with my head in her lap
as my mother spoke quietly, stroking my head,

and I heard every hushed thing she said.
Goodnight mama, says my husband to the baby.
Goodnight daddy, goodnight hippo, goodnight room.
What we choose happens only in one present tense
and I can't explain why this just staggers me.
What did the man on the street mean to say to the moon?

Orphan Letter

Dear bad dreams my sister has dreamed since she was a child

Dear left eye of my sister's after they take out most of the tumor, *I would
      recognize you now* she says when I stand in front of her, but

Dear but

Dear closed hospital, huge hospital
      and stranger at the desk saying *anything you need*

Dear elevators, up up up, and down, down,
Dear painting of a windowsill in Tuscany on the wall
Dear nurses' aides who say *I'm prayin' for y'all*
      shut the lights off, close the door, she's sleeping, she's

Dear bird sounds for the blind
        who must cross this street from the hotel to the hospital,
      Dear terrible birds, crazy birds, invented, unappeasable

Dear what's invented, dear death
Do you remember
My sister dreams the scariest dreams, you have to be
      so quiet when she's sleeping
   because if she wakes she'll wake suddenly and in terror

Dear what is safe, where do you go when you go
Dear question

Lesson

Seals swallow stones sometimes as ballast.
Otters hold hands while they sleep
so they don't drift apart. Do stars really
make patterns, the sisters, the bear?
How long will three etched silver dishes
remain on a step with a sign *this is free*
before someone's whole soul can be gone?
Who measures the depth of the water
that ice from the glacier keeps melting
to feed to the lake that we cross
on the low, rented boat? The ice here
has traveled as snow past the Andes
and hardens as miles, as fields, as peaks,
then melts into streams blue and purer
than air and I place his gold ring
and her watch in a stream but the water
keeps moving beyond them. This way,
someone keeps calling. Meadowlarks, gulls.
Some humpbacks form nets made of bubbles
for feeding; they swim as a group in tight circles,
exhaling till breath digs a well in the water.
Is it the force of their breathing or is it
the silence enclosed by the well they have made
that traps small fish inside? And why?
Whales can live for a hundred years.
They float for hours or days after they die.

Not Why

Mama, my son moans when he dreams again that I'm gone.
His hand on my finger curves into a lock when I stand.

I remember my mother's shape in the darkness
like a pattern, sew it to the quilt, dip the stitch, pull.

Not her smell nor her actual voice when she said she was leaving.
Long ago rustle of now.

And he's sleeping the whole lit known night long,
my fur-feather baby, lobe and lung,
You know I can't stay, you know

I'll be here forever. It was a dream is what I say
when he tells me I left and that the house
became bigger and trapped him inside his room.

Nameless rainmaker, pattern of drops, and all we remember
the story we tell of it after.

The dead in the ground are the dark good shapes,
here by the bed to stay just a little while longer.
His warm one lock of a hand.

Hold harder, oh pure constellation.

How do we die, my son asks one night without context
while we're choosing his five bedtime books.

Mebble

Then happiness became an egg that broke
across our table. Fragments of shell
through which yolk pooled to placemats,
bright goopy gold that filled loose napkin folds
as if all I could wish for from luck.
My three-year-old pulls himself up alongside
to mash peas on his tray and meow at my hand
and command time to follow and stay. *Can I have that
for a minute,* is what he asks now about my wallet,
or a ball, or an eraser, so he can bring them like a word
between his lips. *Will you stay with me for a minute,*
is what he whispers every evening, and then whispers,
one more minute while he stares at a bar on his crib
till his eyelids collapse. The minute is a smell of smoke.
A texture of leaves in a barrel of flame, the rasp
of a match in late sun. Just one, but the days pass
in cages for clouds, or for wayward balloons . . .
a minute's the sound of the egg as it breaks
but its fragments still cleave to the origin shape.
That's a mebble, says my son, about everything.
We sit at the table and count out the ways, our three
lucky stars, our ten lucky stars, we add them to how
many snowflakes it takes to transform the backyard
to a shell. We wanted the mebble, the mebble
was over, the mebble was all we now had.

The Boy with the Bolt

The boy at my poetry reading wants to start a reliquary.
He might be twelve, his belly billowing like a safety
net for his body and his thick, curly hair the color
of Tang. His shoulders have the breadth and weight
of a kitchen cupboard but his voice is a child's,
girlish and mannered. His name is River.

He tells me the bolt he found along the bank of a river
will be the first official piece of his reliquary.
Meaningful objects are hard to come by, he says with a child's
comic gravity, *but I've got this bolt.* Lifesaver-
shaped erasers line the shop counter behind him beside paperweights
of Paris. In the Q&A his cheeks prick a muddled rum color

each time he asks a question, like *What's your favorite color?*
and *Do you believe in numerology?* His mother scolds, *River!*
when he asks my deepest fear, but he waits
for my answer. I want to ask how he knows what a reliquary
is. I want to know what the bolt looks like, if it's right now safe
in his pocket and if the sign it held warned CHILDREN

CROSSING or WIND GUSTS. A child's
deepest fear is not of danger but of loss, though of loss that doesn't color
what comes after. Absence without aftermath. He's so intent on saving
what surrounds him that who he'll be without it must seem, to River,
as abstract as old age—a minor evil that the simplest of reliquaries
could overcome. I want to hold the bolt's small, solid weight

in my hand, hold its useless intention, but people are waiting
to buy my book and tell me how when they were children
they also lost their mothers, as if inside reliquaries
we keep grief, and not the rose-scented and colorless
bones of saints. As if grief could carry us like rocks across a river,
embedded in sediment so we might safely

walk above water. But grief is the water. I have saved
messages from answering machines and a nearly weightless
shred of cork, several post-it notes, and a petal from a river
of curbside cherry blossoms that my father scooped like a child
with both hands to let fly in front of my mother. Moth-colored
powerless petal. And then—isn't a book also a reliquary?

River waits in line to ask what he should put in his reliquary.
Instead of signing my name I list: *a used eraser, a child's watercolor,
and a page from your diary saying you haven't lost anything,
you're safe.*

Things My Father Brought to Buenos Aires

jewelry of my mother's broken years before she died
one skull, maybe of a bird

notebooks with lists of important Spanish phrases
yo soy, the present tense, *eras,* the past

from a page in one notebook, some words in no order:
I remember, forget
she forgot

my mother's paintings

kissing, he wrote on a small scrap of paper
and then on the back, *escondiendo,* to hide

a chandelier

I have thrown out the cards for restaurants
where he wrote *good* or *very good*
or the name of the person with whom he had eaten

I will go, necesito
I will go for a walk

what to do with his glasses, his tweezers
an amethyst

I am going away, I am going
I go away this Friday

a box of keys

what is your age, in the other, the last word is illegible

shells

I did not grow up then

my mother's paint palette

where did your wife grow up

a magnifying glass

I went, I need to go

parts of a watch

snot nosed brat on one scrap, which is what he used to call me
and in tiny printed letters, *caprichoso,* on the back

the skin that I lived in
her bracelets
I always lived in

a beaded purse
I have to go

a red crayon
let me go

Littoral

I let my bed wash into the waves. Into the shallows
the sheets spread and shattered but my bed
was carried farther. From the room where I slept,
I let waves ferry its wrought frame, bolts freed
from the locks like spells. Dreams
dragging after, pulling the nest-colored wrack.
Slowly the wooden boards went, heaved
down the shore before mantels of water
lifted them past, mistaken raft my father wrote
our names across so I would know which board
went where, and how the frame should fit.
I let it collapse. Mattress light as spindrift now
that once was lifted up by men, its crossroads in the ocean
dropped too deep to sway but plunging toward
the thicker cliffs of water. The finials
my mother sketched, the chisel's sound of dust
that split and rimmed the lathe before my father
stained each one and crowned the posts.
Sharp as a heart, the metal ends, the birthday gift
once set on rugs they spread across our lawn and made
with new red sheets that patterned giant peonies.
They led me from the summer doors, and down
the steps, and past the ponds. Sleep, the sound
of bullfrogs or the bees that swept the dead.
It went away. That heavy gift I dreamed on
every night that locked, the bolts like spells,
the wood that fit, instructions I keep
with me. The whole sea where my bed
is at the bottom without size now. Rush, water.

II

Harp Jazz

Is Alice Coltrane dead I asked my friend and he said everyone's dead.
Right. If he was drunk already or if the sedative
was what tricked his feet off bottom steps but I don't think so,
I don't know how his wife died or how he found her.
Someone cleaned. I wish I could hold you right.
Their house had swallowed its quietness. A whole
house of quietness, ingested. I cut the garden down because he asked me to.
Dumped willow and dill and tomatoes into massive brown bags.
Cucumbers split from the heat were as long as my arms.
Do the crickets sound loud to you my friend asked and I said no.
Am I going to get saved from this he asked and I said no.
You want love, I'll give you love. The black cat I hit
on my way to his sister's house kept running after I hit it
although I hit it straight on going sixty. That's a sound
that requires a space in your flesh, to forget.
We set up his tent in his sister's yard
and there were more stars than I've seen in a long time
but not as many as I've ever seen, not that many.
Stay awake he said after I'd taken his sedative
and I told him about the castle that was a prison
and how next to it in the summer the whole town comes out
to watch movies in black plastic chairs. His eyes were wrong.
They had the sadness of an animal. You know, warm like that,
and still running even afterward and at the same pace.
I didn't stop the car because I didn't want to have to touch its fur.
Stay awake all night and talk to me.
Inside the house, his sister's two children
slept in a room below their parents. A family intact
as a snakeskin cast off from the body. Weight of the air,
but that density, rooted and linked, of their each of them sleeping.
We wished for the names of the flint-pitched birds
while I put my hand on your beard which was wire
and on your hand which was a cluster of grapes and on your chest
which went on for so long. You are always someone else.

My blue balloon, my funny friend, my walkabout through palm trees.
How will you narrate what is happening now he asked
as he drew and then changed and then canceled the lines of my body.
And that was almost everything I wanted.
Come, my warm trouble, my good metal bowl. I'll stay awake all night.
For a little while. I don't know how she died. Come into me.

Long as We Both

Because it is a heaviness and takes only the shape of flesh.
Because I never remember what we paid for the house
      or how to use the word *tautology*.
Because in the mornings we speak to it through nicknames
      that morph into other nicknames
      and rhyme with each other and need nothing else.
Because coffee seems essential and is not,
because the survival of the hydrangea seems essential and is not.
Because the box of a television replaced the box of a dollhouse
      where a tiny and serious person had been laid on a bed
      or leaned to bake cake at a stove with the same
      basic proportions as those of a travel-size padlock.
Because proportion had been stirred into the batter,
because the batter was lumpy but the afternoon late
      and we had to eat, didn't we, put the pan in the oven, set the timer.
Because proportion had volunteered
      to be sacrificed; someone after all had to think of the village
      or of the children or of the future or of the good of the whole.
Because the word *or* had no place in the dollhouse
      and the sacrifice of proportion had been basically
      bloodless, despite its immutable flesh shape.
Because I am not the only one to mistake where for who I am,
      the English garden gone coarse with the gray hair of weeds
      and the sea beyond it like a doubt
      or the heat panicked and rippling off parked cars
      and not one shuddering surge would even think to be sacrificed
      for the sake of the little ones, the innocent in their strollers.
Because I am not the only one.
Because the strollers seemed mockingly expensive
      and the house nothing, the house practically free.
Because the word *practically* slid shut over the sea
      like a smell of wood glue.
      Tautology: the study of dragonflies mating,
      tautology: the tenderness I felt for him asleep.

Because I am not the only one, said the dollhouse to the dollhouse, or
        do you take this, yes I take this, or we had to eat, didn't we
        and the shows we would watch about well-meant vampires
        were almost constantly being recorded.
        The premise of x=x filled the garden, improbable, yes,
        but for a moment expected
        and then the sea we didn't see, and then the heaviness
        well beyond measure.
        Take me, said proportion to the minotaur or the sun god
        or to the blade like pure air at the margin of the knife.

And They Lived

I want a story to keep me company while my husband
stares into his phone, beside me in bed. Any story.
That a man named Solon planned the whole city of Athens
while in love with his mother's friend's son. He broke his hand

trying to catch a turtle on the roof of a temple
is what I want to be told while my husband plays scrabble
against any number of people he hasn't seen in years.
Exist for forty points links to *stop* for twenty-five which

he drops into *tranq* for its *q* worth at least half the house.
Slang for a person or thing that will act as a sedative.
Tonight after three episodes of a show about Russian spies
with perfect American accents, I ask if he like peanuts

and he says he *loves* peanuts, and it's as if we've just met
and are fools for each other, still make out on sidewalks at dawn.
Plutarch recounted the life of Solon "at a time when history
was by no means an academic discipline" wrote someone

on Wikipedia, while Solon wrote a law forbidding slaves
from being gymnasts because his mother's friend's son
was a gymnast and a slave and because he didn't
fall in love with Solon back. "It is irrational to renounce

what we want for fear of losing it," wrote Plutarch.
His eyes in a duel with the screen of his phone, my husband asks
what dentist I'll see tomorrow, and two minutes later:
Did I remember to turn down the heat. *Academic, irrational,*

exist for thirty-two, *tranq* for a house with central heating.
Tell me the one about the peanut that choked Plutarch,
tell me about the backflipping slave. Solon invented the euphemism.
Prisons as chambers, policemen as guards. I love you,

I've said, enough times to make history, or join it, and I mean it,
did you turn down the heat. Let's be civilized, said Solon.
And: No man is allowed to sell his daughter unless she's not a virgin.
He made a law forbidding unions that defeat the object of marriage,

but the object of marriage was an acrophobic turtle at a time
by no means known for steep temple roofs. Four days from now
I'm brushing my teeth when my husband says, I don't feel
any love from you at all. Solon would answer this usefully.

He made a law stating that immediately upon marriage,
bride and bridegroom should be locked in a chamber to eat a quince.
Or if not immediately, then four days from now. Count no one happy
until he's dead, said Solon, to the happiest person alive.

If Then

I had not had enough of the counting
of flames, nor of naming the hoops around air.
Which is why I pretended to be thinking about the past
when my husband reached for my hand across
the length of the bed. It was a small distance, but scale
is a tricky thing. It was an antique bed, but when
we sleep, we leave each other completely. Stop

expecting so much from cause and effect and start
expecting desire to shrink like the incredible shrinking man,
which is to say like an improbable hero
who can escape through holes
in the screen of a basement window. Stop expecting.
If blue, then poppy, if cloud, then baby, if wreck,

then all night long. If your husband were not your husband,
you could meet him in a bar shaped like a tiny secret library
and over sweet red wine and raisin-studded biscuits,
say, *Don't speak to me and don't write to me and disappear
from my body*, because he would have asked you
what you truly want, and you would not have known, body

that you are. You, who can barely conjugate the verb *disappear*
in the language your husband might speak if he were not
your husband, improbable hero, if roof made of clay
then light rain on the arches, and a shadow of Neptune
as tall as the castle's first floor. *Easy*, he'd say, *so I'll disappear*.
But if then you climbed onto his motorcycle

and rested your chin on his shoulder while he sped
down a side street, he would begin to sing loudly
like a child in a chorus. What you truly want
is to be the covered distance. By you I mean I.
By you I mean I had not had enough, I
had not had enough, I mean nothing

but that I had not had enough. I name each of the hoops
after changes in weather and the idiosyncrasies
of former lovers, but no hoop knows to come
when it's called. They roll down the hills around town.
They are making a game of my hunger for counting.
They are waiting for the fire breathers and the docile lions.

Whatever You Can

The German psychic healer on the island of Sardinia
said the sack of dry cat food beside her back door
symbolized my ambivalence, then she heaved
the sack into my arms and yelled, *Now let it go!*

But cat food smells even unopened like vomit
and I don't trust cats, so I brought
my ambivalence back to Berlin where
the Jewish Museum was still trying to prove,

through a series of well-designed underground rooms,
that the Holocaust had actually happened.
In one room, the floor had been piled with metal faces,
their features the same but for slight range in size

so that walking across, you can sense how you're walking
on families. Metal on metal beneath me, I clanked
to the farthest dark wall where I picked up the small
metal face of a baby, and let it fall hard on the heap.

A handsome young guard appeared soundless as dew
to call out in a distant if curious tone: *Is there
something wrong with you?* The way boys in high school
would ask with their eyes from the opposite side

of the class, or their tongues—like the time Breck Handy
shoved his in my ear, then returned to his seat
through a havoc of laughs just before Mr. Dickey came in
to begin Ancient History. The rocks in Sardinia

look softer than faces, their shapes turned by waves
into witch hats or candles that reach toward a sea
tinged the same suspect blue as the contacts
I begged for at ten, after words seemed to fuse.

I took off my clothes and walked into the water,
climbed onto a rock that was shaped like a mother
bent over a table, and watched snails scram to the same
exact spots after wave upon wave knocked them off.

Why is she not dead, asked a four-year-old I used to know,
about everyone. My ambivalence is the delicate
Emperor's Hall, unscathed and intact in the bombed-out debris
of its famous hotel, and now kept behind glass

in a mall near the gone Berlin Wall.
It's the pink-tiled ruins of a men's public bathroom
exposed to salt air on Sardinia's shore,
or whatever I see from the edge of an eye

while unlocking the car, the front door
or the drawer with the passports.
I'm so tired around your energy, said the German
psychic healer; *I don't know if I can work with you.*

Die Welt

Past one of the Holocaust memorials I hear someone say
Our stewardess was on Tito's private flight
and she said he was the most charming man.

The stones are different sizes and the ground is also stone
but here it wavers like a blanket or a body.

At night in the bar a man from another country
polishes dark wood saying
I am sorry this cleaning a space before you is not correct.

We live here in Babel with root systems for riverbeds
sculpted from resin, in basins
that fill on a loop in one of the better galleries.

When I ask if he knows how to find the world clock
a man selling hot dogs and dressed like a hot dog
points at me and yells, World clock, world clock, I see you!

But what does unhinged mean, Ricardo asks, and later:
I can't believe how much sadder you are.

Let's just spend the day doing
what normal people do, a woman says to a man
next to the bombed hotel ballroom behind the square of glass.
We don't have to see everything.

In exile you leave the perfect order of Berlin
says the plaque in English
beside another memorial, and in German:
When you leave Berlin, you enter the perfect order.

Photographs don't show how the ground is wrong.

What do you love I ask the man polishing darkness
and he stops, Now that is a difficult question

Lingua

In what shapes do words stay while they wait
to be spoken? *Buonanotte* absorbs into puddles on roadsides,
immune to the grip of *goodnight* on sharp rocks.
Se fossi in te slips through diamonds in chain link
while *If I were you* clings to screens.
The question of what a word means is replaced
by *vuol dir*—what the word wants to say. The word
for why is the word because. A word for love
is also the word for fishhook. The verb *be in love*
is reflexive: *innamorarsi*. To use it we need
a subject, not an object. I myself love. She herself.
She's asleep in the bed as I write this.
On the headboard five stems of yolk-yellow narcissus
run a splatter of shadows along her left arm.
Her elbow extends toward the space I will fill.
Gomito, her elbow. *Gomitolo,* a skein of yarn.
The word in Italian for puzzle is *puzzle*.
We laughed about this on a walk on the banks of the Tiber.
There was still the same star in the sky.
A stunned blue balloon had been trapped by the dam
and it floated the falls in broad rings.
We swallowed its weightless bobbing
in the quick, undoing water. *Pallone,* I said, and pointed.

I Want This till the End

Don't you know your Latin said the poet who wanted to kiss me
repeating *cupio dissolvi* until I wrote the words down

on a placemat. He was taking me out again for dinner.
He was telling me every small thing I should hear. *Grinzosa*

means wrinkled; *beltá* is like beauty but no longer used.
You weren't here, he wasn't you, what's my crime, come on.

It means love for the end is what he tried to explain, but saying
I had to drink more wine because he wanted to.

Eliot called Pound the better locksmith in Italian
although a poet loves inloveness more than any iron gate.

Today's the Day of the Immaculate Conception and so
the locksmith shops aren't open. I had to call a number listed

under SOS after locking myself out of my apartment and when
the locksmith learned that I'd come from the city of Rocky Balboa,

he agreed to stay for a cup of coffee. *Cupio* means wish
but also yearn for and hunger, to covet, to crave and to need.

What's the difference, I asked the poet, between love
for the end and for pretty young bodies—*good question,* he said

and he puzzled like a stoplight, *but there is one, there is one, there is.*
I wanted him to want to kiss me too. The locksmith is a widower.

He never thought his wife would die, not once
in forty years, he said—it just wasn't a thought he ever had.

We agreed at our stupidity but in his eyes was loneliness I didn't want
to recognize; I know he'd feel the same and didn't blame me.

I want to ask the poet what's the difference between beauty
and a beauty that's no longer used, or the difference

between death and to dissolve. These aren't the kinds of questions
I would ask you. Husband, you're the absence of longing.

And I promise I'll grow old and die. And I promise I'll give you my life.

Saints

I changed my mind, said Pam at dinner. *Don't meet him for the weekend.*
This, an hour after she'd insisted she had no advice
although she just turned seventy and Tuesday afternoon
she'll meet the married psychoanalyst in what will be
their only tryst in thirty-seven years of swearing love.
Afternoon, says Pam, because she never leaves the house at night

and won't invent fake plans to tell her husband.
Don't, she said, *because—so many years pass, and things*
just get more disappointing. Her husband came back to the table
with Trader Joe's tart cherry pie. Delicious.
Later when I asked her to remind me why I shouldn't go, she paused
"Masters of Sex" and said, *I changed my mind again,* but had no reason.

Each minute or two minutes I pull out my phone to check
if he's received my last two messages, the first one saying
Please stop, this isn't good for us, I like my life, can't do this now,
the second saying, *Just let me see your face.* Six months this time
not speaking, then in half a day we slipped from my: *Are you in love?*
typed through the phone, to his brief pause, at which I started weeping

but then stopped to let my seatmate off the train.
I'm fucking someone half my age, he texted back, then: *Listen, you're*
a memory, my best, but just a memory, then *you're—,* then *my—,*
and now, his *Come, or I'll come there. We'll choose this or we won't,*
once and for all. Once and for all, the train tracks sing to bits of trash
on platform steps, to whims of light that roam a plastic bag.

I love the flat tops of these rowhomes that pass, how they hold
every loneliness, family, inside, how it's them passing by
and not us on the train, since I'm motionless here and just watching.
Branches in the sunlight like epiphanies.
They could be arrows that don't break Saint Sebastian.
They could be veins in Saint Teresa's face.

Tiresias Too

I'd be a blue whale, said a student in class today,
for the way they travel thousands of miles and months

without needing to eat. I had asked them to go around
sharing their names and then saying into what

they would choose to be changed. *I'm Mira,*
and I would be mist over frost. I'd be a sloth. A lilt.

I'm Mimi, and I want to be a star you can't see.
Like one from all the trillions in the done and gone

that burn above our kitchen where I've come now
in the not-yet-dawn to wait for early morning to erase

too late. Upstairs my husband's sleeping.
The sadness spread between us feels looser

than the slumped brown bird I eased the stroller over
so our toddler wouldn't see. What is it

that I'm doing here? In Ovid's *Metamorphoses,* mute girl
upon mute girl is turned to tree bark or a littered pool

or luckier, a wall of cliff off which the sounds of *What*
and *here* come chiming back as if what makes it broken

is what makes it clear. *I'm Bri,* said Bri, *and I'd be*
surface tension inside water. That force—you know—that keeps

the water drops from sliding off the tops of pennies—how
the thing that really holds them are the drops beneath.

The girls take every kind of shape, a rape victim
or river nymph but why they metamorphose is suspiciously

the same. Beloved to beloved: Saved! So praise
the gods on high, those shits in charge of marriage, beauty.

Who cares about the soul, say all the myths.
Spinoza claimed that prophets speak according

to their temperament—that those who preached
deliverance were also ingrained optimists, and those

who knew the end was nigh were naturally depressed.
Then woe, behold: this wondrous sign, the kitchen lights

won't say. Spinoza spent his short life grinding lenses
so he died that way; his lungs had filled with bits of glass

he'd mixed with grit to flush and smooth till vision
wasn't hope but work, *an admirable polish,* said the man

who first saw Saturn's rings about Spinoza's microscopes:
true sight as something practical to which one simply

shows up every day. *I want to be that thickness in the air
before a massive storm,* one student said, and someone else:

the imprint that a face leaves on a pillow. Befores and afters
held up clear as outlines one could choose. It's nothing

like a bird, our bed, it's not a cliff or wondrous sign
but only what's unknown and so goes looking

for the ending's home. If I could see the future I'd see
nothing more than shapes that change; I'd go upstairs

right now and put my arms around his chest, and press;
I'd make him laugh. But prophecies are loyal to the past.

Moses thought that human beings weren't meant to see
the face of God and therefore, said Spinoza, God obliged him.

Tiresias too, lucky mythical bastard: blind as a bedsheet,
blind as the storm-throttled air. Go upstairs. God gave me

his name, Moses told the believers. God gave me a rock.
I want to be all the hopeful gone faces that watched.

III

Variorum

All the pretty girls.
Parsley, sage, salt, glue.
And you're a big help to him
says my husband's father
when I share his news of promotion.
Hey, hey, buckle my shoe,
No sing me a new song mama
says my son before bed.
All the pretty girls.
No another song.
Lost my partner what'll I do,
lost my partner what'll I do.
Skip to my lou my darling.
No a new song.
Hey little girl is your daddy home
did he go and leave you all alone
I got a bad desire.
Where am I going with this
I'm thinking while he watches
his pillow to picture the words.
All the pretty girls.
He fucked the shit out of her explained
my father about the plot of a movie.
The pretty girls.
Dad do you have to say that to me?
Mama another one. Mama a new one.
Well I'm sorry but that's what he did.
You're a big help to him.
All the pretty girls.

In the Middle of the Myth

I am tired of the plot, said the river.
Sometimes the hero stares at my rippled changing
and sometimes she throws herself into me.
Save her, don't save her, I am tired
of how the plot pauses at the question
as if it's come to an end. Come to an end!
The change in me moves without music.
Sometimes, sometimes: disjunctive sound.
Sometimes she falls unutterably in love
the way deer leap across me not breathing.
The pause in the plot was a furred white star
on the rib of a deer disappeared now.
I am tired of now and was. Now I circle the castle
of happily after, castle of moment as myth.
Now she washes her face with the whole of me
before climbing the threshold of steps
to then pivot and jump. Her hopelessness
separates into the gleam on silt.
I carry her masked fish smoothness
to the black root shape she wants to mimic.
I carry her limbs down to root hair and rock.
Call it lifesaving, call it nature, call it
the purity of luck. I have never liked the body.

Cinerem

with definitions taken from a page in Anne Carson's Nox

The residue from a fire; ashes (we stayed
in hotel rooms in different cities); ashes
of various materials (in bed once he blessed
every part of my body); oxide of copper;
(*blessings on your thumbs* he said like a high priest
in his own other language); the extinct or apparently
extinct ashes of a fire (I once knelt at a magnolia
because the magnolia was blooming);
residue (and behind me he was breathing)
from a fire; ashes (he breathed what I'd breathed,
wanted each of my longings); hot ember
by which (*why does the petal smell like lemons*
is what he asked me) the spent or smoldering
"fires" of love (if I said I remember his voice
I would be lying); hot ember by which
(once he stabbed me with a fork in my gum
while I was talking); oxide of copper
(one of the tines broke the skin and my gum
started bleeding); ashes regarded as (*blessings
on your neck, on your breasts*); the result
of waste or destruction (if I said I remember
I would mean I am covered in fish gills); ember
(I would mean we are water and we are moving
through water); of copper (and he knew
how to suck all the sacred up); ember
(and I sucked all the sacred up with him); by which
(I am saying I didn't doubt it); the bitter ash
of men and nights (he was a mean man.
he was a devil in the myth that I placed in the water);
of waste (I am saying he was a story, an edge
with no falling); whether cremated or not
(I could write on his chest, *you're my cloud,*

passing over); the spent or smoldering fires
of love (and I know about boredom); or a stage
in existence (and I know about choices)
ashes of various materials (don't think I'm not happy);
as in the extinct (although I could now call him
I don't call him); ashes of a fire (or I could just
hear his voice) of love (I would like to hear his voice);
residue. Ashes as a condition of the body.

Who the Letters Were From

This guy I used to know—a friend of mine—my
ex-husband I met at nineteen on a blind

date though I could see by the time
our fried clams had arrived it wasn't meant

to be—he said time would only
tell—I said meantime I'll only be

wishing you well but when
the check came he was a different

man—I mean he was my student—or I
his and he was obviously an expert in early

sixth-century anonymous Gaelic poetry
that revolves around a rhyme scheme—

as he explained over the beer we shared illegally
after class—in which changing the placement

of any one word means reducing
the poem to nonsense. He was good

with his head—or hands—or at nothing
but baking bread although when all was said

and done he remained a rabid Catholic
who wanted to ban the word embryo

or he was having an emotional affair
with a pregnant woman and loved jawbreakers

and whether I ran into him at Walmart
or we went intentionally to the river is beside

the point because he was a black hole
which meant not actually on earth and therefore

could only be known as the Dark Lord (his name
was Josh) or the World's Most Apologetic Liar

or the illustrious co-author of *How to Surmise
Then Hypnotize Your Real Mr. Right* and we spent

a single night together without technically
inhaling but the divorce still proved undoing

for the children. He was the father
of my dictionary. He was an irreplaceable

rhyme for baby. He was my third
love, my second chance, a trampoline's notion

of romance. Maybe now, maybe then,
maybe if, or so the end refrains. He was one

of a number of mistakes I made
for which I don't take blame.

The Next to Last to First Kiss

Happened on a Saturday night at songwriting camp
and remained fateful for months afterward
because he carried my hand to his mouth
and pressed startling lips to say *Remember me*
in a language we didn't yet speak. I remember
the dormitory rec room and wall-sized windows,
that fast-swimming whale of my own secret self.
Not him. His hair might have been curly,
he might have had a voice like apples falling
onto a table and a crooked way of leaning to ask
for my name. For some time after, I thought
we might get married, though I met him
only once. Oh fate you are the glorious
queen of the prom. I vote for you over and over.
The next kiss tasted of Sprite, came on a dare
in a parents' garage. The next kiss came in a white
nightgown in Europe on a wooden floor, came
on a porch in Texas through purple night air
where for weeks I walked careful as crumbled-up chalk.
The next kiss was pulled out of me
by a single finger hooked into the side of my mouth.
The next kiss was littered with vomit and laughter.
The next kiss tasted like cigarettes and endings
that had been buried under pennies. The next kiss
was the last kiss. It followed me down back roads
at midnight in Asia. Shadowless cows pretended
to sleep while it cornered me in attics and temples.
The next kiss was strangled by cattails.
I wrapped it in tea muslin for the funeral
that was scheduled for winter but lasted all spring.
The next kiss held back like static on the radio.
The next kiss was made out of nothing
but August and slipped through car windows

to hitchhike back home. Signless and trusting
it waited on the roadside for each passing sureness
to offer a ride. Fateful for months, fateful for days,
fateful for lip-sealed minutes. The first kiss wished
through the whale of self to a what-iffed list
as precise as the salt in the sea. Remember me.

When the turbulence ends

it is not a clear sky
that will land the plane safely
but fully forgetting what wind shear
first made it lurch.
You can't treat me this way, someone texts,
and a pigeon in love with another pigeon
takes a shit on the chimney
outside my window.
They spend sunsets up here,
the two pigeons, nuzzling beaks
into necks fat with feathers
that glint, at that hour, like oil slicks.
I don't know what the pigeons see in each other
or if they've finally begun to get bored
after what could be more
than four hundred years
in pigeon time
or if I should text back saying, *How?*
or, *You can't treat me this way either*
or, *It's as if the pigeons' feathers,*
nestled at sunset together,
want to reflect the great oil slick of the sky.
I can, in fact, treat you
exactly this way.
The bloom's off the rose,
the glint's off the feathers, the charm's
off the ding of the treasured text message.
Once dried, their shit takes on the tint
of the pigeons.
When the turbulence ends,
it doesn't matter who loved
or who didn't
or who said what they said
about whose heart

being like lice—
that is, harmless, and itchy,
and everywhere.
Blame grabbed a cloud
that the plane rode through
and blame stayed there.

Pay the Ransom

Like a mean trained dog desire searches through your body.
It ignores the blade of snow across the rooftops.

Sighs cut out of chimney smoke pull slightly at your hair.
They taste the way his beard tastes when you suck them.

Desire cocks an ear and hears the snowy rooftops dull
into a mild, less white whiteness, though

its enemy of memory still doesn't stand a chance:
Danny Dunham's teenage hand against your teenage head

until you knelt in someone's yard in South New Jersey.
You've never even been to South Jersey.

Four flights down, families amble between churches
in the oldest town in Europe, pressing tiny buttons on their phones.

Swallows fly south, then north, then settle
like a change of heart along a rooftop.

My clear then obscure and then clear again treasure, is what
he writes: *I'm a small-time thief and you've already been kidnapped.*

The blue shutters of regret stand guard over windows.
You're as patient as a waterfall, or as neon losing luster.

The *T* of your name is a word that means you. *Ti amo,*
ti voglio un sacco di bene, vorrei respirarti, va là. You will go

home with your husband and the thick idle reed of your house
will grow tall by a river. Your body is a jar of hours.

Statues of the virgin inside churches beg forgiveness
for your perfectly sturdy curving. The rooftop snow

has been swallowed or fisted
into the feathered uncolor of night.

That'll Teach You

There was, in fact, an end to desire.
It took a hammer and several hideous small towns
but by the time they had gotten
within miles of the sea,
she could think of him as blunt, and almost rotten.

He kissed her in the motel lobby
which was the size of a car and said,
I love you do you believe me. What she said in response
was hung by an absurdly heavy room key.
Mere miles, but the bus route

was complicated: from here to the shoreline
the stained concrete buildings were nothing
but frames for dirt fields. And the route's
lack of sidewalk was treacherous. *Not worth it,*
as he often repeated to the back of her neck.

By now the many warnings they had previously encountered
were furious. (The sudden hail, for instance,
when they walked through any church door, or the boy
with no parents who came to find them on a train.)
He said, *You can't have everything,*

but she could, so she allowed him into her room.
Neither of them thought of the sea.
The motel's low hallways had been painted
with mermaids constricted by fishnets,
but no one in that whole town thought of the sea.

The mermaids' eyes looked like pushpins.
It seemed she had failed to reassure them by saying,
*I'll be happy with the top of his head, or a hand, or a finger
from that hand in my mouth.* Each part of his body
had waited patiently for its turn, but the fact remained

that if she had tried to get out from beneath him,
she would not have succeeded. And if she had screamed,
but what, so instead let his tongue slop the rim of her mouth.
She hadn't known what she'd wanted until she stopped
wanting was a more popular theory

among those circulating between the old men
in neighboring rooms, but the shit brown bedspread
had its own theory, which was that everything
would change if he were inside her. *I'm not here,*
she told him, without allegiance to her body,

and he said, *Here or not, it doesn't matter. That'll teach you.*
The difference between kissing and tearing his ear off
had become unforgiving. His ugliness
was so plain as to be dazzling,
although that, too, they would have to forget.

The Night I Slept with My High School English Teacher

I want to begin this story where it ends.
He drops me at the station in the rain before dawn
and says well, should I kiss you goodbye.
His eyebrows rise into the boredom of his body
the way they'd rise in class when someone
suggested Leopold Bloom was homosexual.
All over New Jersey it's raining. He is speeding
to the train, thinking if he can get me there on time
he will not have to wait, and I do actually mistake
a blurry streetlamp for the moon and nod *yes*
to the kiss as if he'd offered it. At the end
I'm a helmet of ambivalence. All transparent shield,
all bulletproof bubble, the vast yes and no of pure metal.
In the middle I can't sleep so I suck on his cock.
It stays limp in my mouth as desire like venom
seeps into the past where I sat on the vast other side
of his desk to talk about my future and his wall
made of books cut a path through the sea back to Ithaca.
Now around us the bodies of sixteen-year-old boys
are asleep on both floors of the dorm and his cock
is a mumbled apology for whatever they did or did not
want from me in the middle of the story as the story
goes: I don't go to that school anymore, I am as old
as Isabel Archer, Dorothea Brooke, the end
of books. It's morning, my ticket in hand.

But I Didn't Look at Her

Hashtag me too, said the man in the next booth, and the two men beside him started laughing. The waitress with menus laughed too. The bald man in a blazer placed his thumb on her lower back—lightly, like pausing a sentence. *I can't resist,* I said, walking over. *Tell me what's funny.* The waitress turned away as if programmed to do so; one pivot, so quick she seemed just to have been passing by. The men laughed harder. *Uh-oh,* said the bald one, touching my back in the same spot: *We're in trouble!*

I placed my palm on his head. *Really,* I said. *I want to hear.* Grinning. *Let's tell her,* said the first man, and he started a story about hot butter, but the bald one interrupted: *She IS mad.* I rubbed his warm head as if soft wood I was sanding and asked, how could I be mad at someone so gorgeous. He asked if I was joking. Crouching, I grabbed some fat on his waist, and tugged. *I bet your penis is huge,* I said. The first man yelled, *It is! It's this big!* He picked up a bottle of hot sauce. *Oh, his penis is bigger than that,* I smiled, then whispered: *I bet you're good in bed.* He stood up. Shaking his jacket for a cigarette that wouldn't drop. *I can't tell if you're joking,* he said, then he walked out of the restaurant. Now the third man in the booth, the one who hadn't spoken, pointed at me with that pistol gesture to mean, right you are, or, gotcha. I pointed the pistol back. Then I aimed my hand toward his lap, and the look on his face changed.

Let's start over, said the first man. He was here for the Super Bowl, he'd come from Columbus, Ohio, and where was I from, and what was my name. But the quiet one said, No, he was here for work, they were colleagues. They work as inspectors of fire trucks.

I went to the bar and paid the waitress, but I didn't look at her. The man with the bald head or penis stood outside smoking, and either telling the doorman what I'd said or not, but I kept walking, and thinking how in various versions of this story, I'm the one who seems insane. But I felt simple. Like if your first grade teacher asks what's two plus two, how confusing it would feel to say sixteen, or nine hundred. I wanted to rub it much harder. For a second I just started pushing his head back and forth.

Claudio Says

Claudio says those photos of Mussolini covered the wall
of that bedroom when he bought the place.
The back part here where the whorehouse was
is a hotel now. For people who want adventure,
he adds, winking at my husband with his one good eye.
Claudio's hair looks like a hologram, glimmering
into a wave of rust-colored hair dye.

He says last night his friend came to eat here
and his friend is eighty-one and an honest-to-God communist
and said he'd never vote for that politician with the earring.
Maybe this country's leader is passing shit laws, Claudio says,
but blame him for that if you want to blame him,
not for being seventy and liking the pussy.

He shows us the page in a book of favorite quotations
where Enzo Ferrari claims Claudio's wife
makes the best tortelli in Italy. Claudio says
he once got a rooster to fall in love with a cat.

In one of the photos, Mussolini is shirtless and reaping corn.
The handwritten caption reads "Duce, the great farmer."
Claudio says the stained-glass windows in all the bedrooms
are original, but he himself installed mirrors above all the beds.
On the laundry line at the edge of a field, a bathmat
hangs to dry beside a women's flannel nightgown.

A Section from the Myth about Psyche and Cupid

in memory of Jyoti Singh, 1990–2012

The teenage boy who raped a woman in the back of a bus
and then pulled her intestines out through her vagina
has learned to paint. What's the right order of that sentence?
What I wanted to say: his painting, entitled *The Princess*,
has won a prize. He lives in a prison for teenagers now
and they're learning to cook, and to paint.
The Princess wears a regal blue robe, says the newspaper,
and she is looking into an ornate mirror on the wall.
There were others with the boy; you know what they did.
The sentence goes: She was the most beautiful girl in the world
and her beauty was known throughout the land
and she lived for two more weeks in the hospital
and told the police clearly what happened.
The veil that flows from the Princess's crown is lemony yellow
and it billows beyond the frame drawn with a black ballpoint pen.
This and then this, she said, but the doctor explained
to her father that the insides of her body were no longer there.
Says the lawyer, defending: "A 'lady,' or 'girl' —
these are more precious than diamonds.
You want to keep a diamond in your hand.
You put your diamond on a street, the dog will take it."
The Princess reflected in the mirror
is not quite the same as the Princess who looks back.
Different length hair, for example, and different face.
The one looking is touching her reflection,
while in the mirror her hand is at her throat.
"There is no trace of anger in him," observes the psychologist.
The mirror is made of barrow bird feathers.
The mirror is made of bricks. Of gold eyes. The mirror
is the door to the castle, come in. All hail. You are the one.

Poem without Antigone

And I was again a girl among many,
the verb through which I existed
        having been translated from a past
so definitively past that the dead
        felt no need to apologize.
History like a pigeon among pigeons
        on a street by the shore where I was a girl.
Among many, our fingernails sand-packed
        and covered the color of shadows
from beaches we dug through to reach
        the earth's core, where good golden hair
grew like patience defeating escape.
        History pecking hard flakes
of a brioche, history scattered by toddlers.
        I was again a girl, and everywhere
I placed the stilled verb of my gaze,
        water formed a wake that both framed
and delayed its departure. Goodbye,
        self, goodbye frothed lip of the rippling
narrative surface. I was, I was, everywhere
        I was. Everywhere I was, the girls' eyes
gleamed like beads on an abacus.
        Many and one stacked half against half
and the scale slid inward and jammed.
        In a day we could dig into the shore
beside our mothers down to towers
        that rose in a chorus of bricks on which
cobwebs had crosshatched our names.

IV

Where to Put It

The room in which I start sobbing again and wonder
if my sobs will hurt the baby inside me, and the room
in which I hope so, a room made entirely of a window.
                    The room of my husband's goodnight,
which is a room in a large municipal building with Styrofoam ceilings
where lines must be formed so forms can be signed, a room
surrounded by parking lots, and he knocks opening its door
and says, *You can't be this sad for the next five months—it's not tenable.*
                    The room overlooking the perfectly circular hole
in our street that's at least ten feet deep and no neighbor
knows when it appeared or if there's a reason.
                    The room in which instead of eating dinner
I drive for hours past porches where women with voices
like hammered fenders call out baseball scores
into the peeled blue air that will not link itself to a season.
                    The room in which a man the color of sand
stands on a median toward the end of dusk with a sign saying
he has children and will do anything
and the room of the cars before lights turn green.
                    The room in which we are filled with longing
like a wave too large. *Do you see me* is what we can't find words to ask.
                    The room in which a new student shows up
for my poetry class for formerly homeless people who are mentally ill
and she has my mother's smile.
                    The room in which so many women
have my mother's smile: women entering restaurants, women
standing at counters with handfuls of change.
                    The room of the dream in which the baby
is my mother and I am the vent between a sidewalk and steam.
                    The room in which I tell my father,
I miss Mom so much I can't think about her and the room in which
he answers back, *Me too,* lit as it is by the end of dusk as the cars
pass through when the stoplights turn; now the man's sign drops, I'll
do anything.

The room in which my father is living
with a woman younger than I am and the room in which he is my father
and the corridor between them down which no one walks,
and *Do you see me, Yes I see you,* and *Do you see me, No I'm lonely,*
and the room of my seventy-year-old father
and his seventy-year-old friends pretending to trip each other and laughing,
                and the room in which they're invisible, age like the white ceiling
and white walls, the window dissolved to a water-shaped memory of touch.
                The room in which I ask the no-longer-homeless woman
what the poem about kindness is about, and she says it's about anger,
says this with my mother's smile, the smile of my mother's illness
that could have decimated grown men in agreement with each other, and did.
                The room in which the woman's smile becomes
an ordinary moth that lifts off the table and slips through a hole
in the star-cracked slats of the ceiling's foam—Are we
sharing a space, do you see me.
                The room of the water-shaped tenable.
                The room in the house, the lit room upstairs, books on the shelves
by the window, the room we drive by in the nighttime, someone inside.

Dome of the Rock, Rock of the Tunnel

My husband sighs into the dark to complain
    he can't sleep and his blame
        has the small, inconspicuous shape
    and scant weight of a bookmark.
        Downstairs the alarm whines in starts

as his father keeps trying and failing to set it.
    It's like in a crazy house, my husband says.
        Take this blame, it's a little pebble.
    Take this blame, it's a tunnel that goes
        to the other side of the rock.

Imagine, I said to my student, if I were to tell you
    I was born in a city that's reached by a tunnel
        whose portal was painted
    to look like a rainbow, and it leads
        through a cliff and on top of the cliff

is a massive state prison that no one beyond it can see.
    My student was trying to describe what he saw
        when he pictured the city
    his family could no longer live in.
        I had heard his same language before

so did not hear it now.
    In the city of his family: a gold dome,
        and around the dome: a wall.
    So tell me about the wall, I said to my student.
        So then tell me about the concrete.

Poems are handfuls of dirt that you scoop
    from the ground near your home,
        wrote a poet whose body
    has never been found, but it's handfuls of dirt
        that are handfuls of dirt. The blame

is a dome, or a knot. My husband says
        we'll be okay, said a white woman in the gift shop
                when I read from my phone that the president
        just banned three news outlets from the White House.
                How much is this stationery with the swirling.
                How much for this one with the cats.

Tell me about your city, the dirt there.
        No, tell me about the gold dome
                beneath which the American dream
        beats wings like fists through the sealed air
                of superlatives. It was never my dream,

said a Black woman in the gift shop
        buying glitter and spools of silk ribbon.
                Right, I said. Like that video yesterday
        of the thirteen-year-old boy who kept saying
                Just let me go

and the cop dragging him through front yards
        saying, I'm not gonna let you go,
                and then dropping the kid in some bushes
        and pulling his gun out.
                Right, I said, but by saying

he's a thirteen-year-old Mexican boy
        and the cop is this white guy with a shaved head.
                Language hasn't migrated yet,
        hasn't reached where we are.
                So we haven't reached where we are.

The boy, the Mexican-American kid, the thirteen-year-old's
        stepfather is a cop.
                After the white cop with the shaved head
        pulled the gun on him, the boy
                was arrested. Wait, what?

said the white woman in the gift shop when I told her
        CNN, the New York Times. What?
                I had heard her same language before
        so did not hear it now. The wall was just plain,
                I guess grayish, explained my student.

But that gold of the dome. Dome
        of the rock, rock of the tunnel
                that leads from the city that built
        the gray wall around memory's
                migrating dirt. After the cop pulled the gun

but before no charges were filed against him,
        people broke windows of a home
                they mistook for the cop's home;
        an old woman lived there. Christian, that's
                the boy's name. And the cop, his name

is Ferguson. San Francisco, Jerusalem, Anaheim.
        Those who migrate are inventors.
                I know, said a different white woman
        in the gift shop. I already freaked out this morning.
                So I did not hear it now. My husband

was in the military, so he knows, and he said.
     So we haven't reached where we are. I am here
          because I am scared, said the poet, after naming
     the handfuls of dirt but before he was buried
          without any trace in the ground near his home.

Maybe you are, too. Maybe you are
     Mexican-American, African-American, Native
          American, my president, the president, my
     husband said. Language the bones in the wings of the fists.
          Let me go, it's easy. Just take your hands off me.

The Absolute Door

is not the door to go through.
Don't look for the box in the closed antique shop
with the warped copper latch and the sign
carved on top saying start over.
Steer driftingly clear of the peaked foreign town
in the north where the sun is a scratch.
Death: not relevant. Nor will you get
to keep one of your ten truest stories.
Sing the alphabet backward in accents
of animals, holding the hand of your son
as he crosses each street. Oh the glorious more
of your patient wrong feet as you walk
to the Afterwords Bookstore.
Joy like the water-wrecked light
at the bottoms of bridges.

Take It Everything

The light before nine at night in the Roman ghetto
is a light we would find at the bottom of lakes

if like fish we could live without lungs to pump air.
God might have made fish to be heavy as lead,

said Galileo, but he wanted to teach us about ease.
Families have gathered at outdoor tables

to eat warm cheese on warm bread with their fingers.
An old man in an apron smiles like several fields

to an old man with two bills in his hand. *This for me?*
asks the man in the apron, tossing up English like fruit

that he's just learned to juggle. *This for you,*
is the answer he's given: *Take it, everything!*

In Italian there's a tense for a past so far past
that most people forget how to use it. It's a tense

for a past that has no direct link to right now.
Six hundred years ago in a prison beneath a castle

built into the bed of the Bay of Naples, a monk
spent three decades in water that reached to his knees.

For ink he squeezed blood out of cockroaches
to write: *The world is a grand and perfect animal*

and: *Each piece of dirt is alive.* With deck chairs
they drag from their kitchens at dusk, widows cluster

on bricks that are lit with the light inside lakes.
Their bodies are certain as books. He could have built

bones for the birds out of gold, Galileo explained, and made
their veins of living silver. The old man in an apron

sits down at my table, says: *Here you are welcome,*
whatever you want—you are guest of the house tonight.

The Poem about Chuck E. Cheese
a Friend Posted on Facebook

was not about the Chuck E. Cheese across the parking lot
from Target where we celebrated my son's fifth birthday
yesterday, though the poem was "a fucking masterpiece"
according to the friend who posted it and who, as it happens,

is an expert on masterpieces, having trained
to decipher the love letters, poems, and sacred
decrees that for nine hundred years have been stuffed
in a synagogue's attic in Cairo because they contain

the word god, or g-d, as my Orthodox student
wrote in her sestina about last week's dismantling
of an illegal Israeli settlement. My son's birthday party
was not celebrated in the attic of a synagogue

but at what the poem on Facebook describes as
"the diabolical vampire of our transcendent ideals."
What I know about transcendent ideals wouldn't fill
one of the rubber finger puppets you can choose

from the cheaper prizes but rather it starts and ends
with the sound of my son's voice in the bathroom
of Chuck E. Cheese as he lovingly whispers to no one
while peeing, *I wish my home was here.* Wistful as faraway kites,

or as mist near an island. My son turned five on the fifth
anniversary of the death of a boy who had gone out
to buy skittles. "White people," instructed Black people on Facebook
while a table of five-year-olds in rat hats waited for a band

of animatronic rodents to play Happy Birthday to my son,
"Say something about him." That he went to aviation camp
and liked math more than English, that he had
this lit jewel of a face. *Can you see someone when they're dead,*

my son asked last week, and also if police would take his bunny
from our car when we went to the bakery. *What do police DO,*
he wants to know. Our lies are a ball gown in layers of tulle
made for posing on carpets the color of state your name here

and explain why you came to this country. *They pull people over,*
answered Sammy from my son's class while we drove home
from the party and then added, *They don't like when you call them
the po po. This Chuck E. Cheese is better than the scary Chuck E. Cheese,*

he said, and I asked what happened at the scary one.
They . . . bit a human there, he said, and then: *a real human.*
They bit a human there? I asked. *A person . . .* he said, *a people . . .*
They cut off the head of a . . . someone who is real.

Last night the news praised one journalist as "a hero
for democracy," and since I am on a mad and intermittent hunt
for heroes of democracy, I looked him up and found a photo
of his head placed on his torso in the desert. A real . . . people.

From the attic of a synagogue in the old part of Cairo,
my friend studies day wages, grocery lists, oaths,
and a twelfth-century rabbi's banned *Guide for the Perplexed.*
No one's head has ever been cut off at Chuck E. Cheese,

Sammy, I promise you, I told him, but the word for forgiveness
in Byzantine Hebrew shares roots, wrote the rabbi
on chalk-whitened goat skin, with the Arabic word for impossible.
My brother told me, replied Sammy. *He said it's true.*

It Doesn't Matter

If your grandfather beat your uncle and impregnated
the neighbor, or if at eleven your mother swallowed a bottle
of his barbiturates, and your grandfather kept her awake all night
mopping the kitchen floor while he talked to her about poems
and his steamship during the war, or if your grandmother
finally left him for a man wanted by the FBI
and they hid for years in a house in the Bayou before he left
without saying goodbye, or if your mother's first marriage
at nineteen was the work of a voodoo doll named Matilda,
or if, at ninety, your grandmother lost the ability to speak
and broke the ends of words open into the sounds
of a mechanical sheep, or if the patience of the ocean is any saltier
than its rage and what blunt need to make the past mean
more than it means do we tend like skin when what persists
is as unrecognizable as the turn from *that* it happened to *if*.
If your mother was unanimously voted Homecoming Queen
or your uncle died toothless with guns in folded sweaters
or if the house built from redwood that he'd salvaged from old barns
has somehow gotten smaller, or if in the fields beyond it,
wheat where you played swords with your cousins has grown taller
than knees, and its blades lunge forward like bison in a stampede
and if beyond the fields are cliffs but beyond the cliffs
are the white mouths of waves that no one can reach.
Wildflowers grow out from the face of those cliffs:
poppies, dandelions, and wild lupine whose blooms
seem an almost chemical shade of purple, so absolute
and incontestable that if you were to puncture a petal,
time itself would spill out and ask you for proof.

The Night My Father's Parents Left Him in a Park

was not yet night. Dressed in the good wool shorts
that scratched his knees, my father

pushed his little brother on a swing while dusk
smirked through the rungs of a jungle gym.

He counted to ninety-nine and back down again,
ten times. My name is Gabe, he repeated,

and we are in Hollenbeck Park, in the city
of Los Angeles, where we live. When he pushed

the swing faster, his little brother's laughter
pressed into the pulse of his throat. My brother

is four years old, he told the swing, and his name
is Mo. Ninety-one, ninety, eighty-nine. He began

to understand: no moment in time
is returned to. That they had grown into boys

aged four and five, or that they'd been brought to play
in their best clothes, or that each ledge of dusk

would first come, then go: fact after stunningly
haphazard fact, and not one could be undone.

Dusk fastened itself onto cars that sped
like UFOs or confused shooting stars past the park.

If someone would hold his hand, he could cross
the street, and if he could cross the street,

he could bring his brother home. This logic
seemed to frustrate the rungs of the jungle gym.

The night was a brick house in the future
but the white car headlights of actual fear

kept on speeding right past the park's border.
Beyond it his mother was screaming at his father

in a cut-pebble mixture of Yiddish and Polish
which my father had not been taught and thus

would not ever know if she was screaming
We've forgotten them or, *They had to go.*

My name, said my father to the new house
of night, is Gabe. The hurt, curdled sound

of his mother's voice somehow trapped
on my father's tongue made him shrug.

He would have to bring his little brother home.

The Delta

The dark gold bark of the crepe myrtle
curves like the arms of Inés's younger daughter
who pushes a stroller past roots that have ruptured
the Tigre's old sidewalks. It's New Year's Day, again,
and families picnic by the delta whose green water eases past
the gated homes of former torturers, and signless summer camps
on peeling stilts. Time is a broken invention and ought
to be placed underneath the locked safe behind coats
in between the toy cars and tin robots my father collected.
Boys along the riverbank are lifted over young men's heads
to whack at balls, and miss, and fall down happy.

Here when a child gets lost, whoever spots them
starts to clap, and other strangers stop to clap along
until the strip of beach, or mall, becomes a crowd
of loud applause the mother hears, and knows
where she can find them. On the drive from the city, my son
placed his head in the palm of my hand, then put himself to sleep
by singing songs about belugas in blue seas.
Past the highway, slums receded: stacked huts
blurred like galaxies while sleek red blooms on ceibo trees
announced the quiet side streets. Mimosa, agapanthus,

jacaranda. Look at that crepe myrtle's carpet of petals,
I tell Inés whose older daughter is dead
and she tells me about the mushroom-shaped mansion
behind them, how the son of the famous painter who built it
lived for ten weeks on the flesh of his friends
after their plane crashed in a snowdrift in the Andes.
The famous painter asked a psychic who had grown up fixing watches
if his son was still alive and every time the psychic looked,
his answer shifted. *We come back home*
are different words in every language: my son is asleep, now I
am the mother—broken numbers, silver and delicate clock face.

What You Don't Remember

You lost your own house once, standing in front of it
during a snowstorm. A large lake of a house, locked
rooms cold as stones but for one where you slept
by a cast-iron stove and your parents
who never would leave you. What wish
sent you out to the hollowing skull bone
of snow? You'd been told how all flakes
make their own matchless patterns
and, patient, you watched for each one.
The yard yawned its end into hills thick as books
that your mother had filled with fall leaves.
You walked through time and past it
while snow waited, its sound like the sound of wings
on sleeping birds, of paper being crushed underwater.
Out of time, the air stitched itself up
into icy sweaters, feathers, a spin of walls.
You were the quiet you heard. Kitchen windows
dissolved into holes in the snow that then
folded and filled as if no unique pattern could matter.
The house swayed to wobble, tipped. You swished
in your coat hood without it. You were not
trying to find your way. You were not afraid.

Philtrum

/'filtrəm/ the vertical groove on the surface of the upper lip, below the nose.

I

Paper boat, rift
in the water.

Deft bluff
of a thumb.

Misplaced teardrop,
left to dry.

Cool cleft
of the river bed.

II

Before we are born, the angel of God comes to the womb
and teaches us everything. How the lung books in scorpions
let them breathe, the nature of a galaxy's greed.
Whole memories, and the words for each piece of the world.

Then birth. And the angel returns as our mothers
begin to suffer, silences cells as our mothers beg.
Push, someone urges, and *almost,* while inside,
the angel traces a finger from the nose to the top lip, so when

we enter our lives, all we were taught is forgotten.

III

Inside my mother I knew the shape and history of the tundra.
I knew the sound of mollusks as they fidget into pearls.

I knew how the color blue was made,
and why the ocean didn't trust it.

I knew the shy longings of salamanders. I knew
the symphonies turtles heard, in some afternoon dreams.

I knew each dream of death and its fish shape, its lopped
and odorless trace. Sometimes I played them like dominoes.

Sometimes I marched the future onto windowsills, propped
certain summers like painted soldiers, to protect imaginary streets.

Sometimes I sang Frank Sinatra into the thought of seedpods.
I hummed my mother's lullabies into the thought

of morning glories, then I whistled
into the thought of them dying as the day wore on.

I poured time into the thought of milk saucers, and I lapped it.
I swallowed the thought of rocks.

IV

Envelope
for the kiss.

Spoon
of scent.

It culls
the breath

from lovers,

lulls
them in.

V

When I knew everything, those few wrong days
that waited sleepless in the future

—walking home from the neuro-oncologist's, or
the blunt surprise taste of the older boy's thumb—

those days furled into days surrounding to become
a single conch shell. I held the thought of this shell

and listened to its sea sound, combers
simmering into sun from the salt surface of sea.

VI

Only the angel regretted it, taking the knowledge back.
I didn't want to keep what I had learned.

Nor did I want to lose it. But I did not mumble *Wait,*
in that language an angel understands.

And I did not feel bereft when the knowledge left me,
when forgetfulness filled into oxygen, pulling the veins.

The angel grazed a finger across my face,
soothing a groove into the plain of skin. *That*

was what I wanted: to be touched.

Now You Can Join the Others

I took absence down to the ocean
and because it is blind, I told it about the waves.
I held its warm hair. When it wept I placed my arms
around the wind shape of a cliff and felt for edges.
Beside it I walked in the streets late at night
and I let it tell me stories. Child who is learning
I said to absence, but I kept it near me as if I were the child.
When it went on its boat into the darker simple water
I didn't look back: I know absence, I thought,
although on the shoreline earlier it had been singing
a song I didn't know. I told it about the graveyard
on top of the mountain but absence cannot see,
cannot picture anything about windchimes above two stones.
Two stones, it sang to the waves, not waiting for me.
I walked with it to the bridge and then to the next
bridge and I stayed like a shawl over the cliff
when we held each other. Wait I said to absence. It looked
like my father. It looked like my mother.
Have you become them I asked and the waves
made their covering motion. I held its hair,
new salt and sand taste no one's hair. Waves arrive
one after another I said. They must be very cold.
They come from far away and bring all of their patience.

acknowledgments

Thanks to the following journals where some of these poems first appeared: *AGNI; Alaska Quarterly Review; The Awl; Crab Orchard Review; Five Points;* the *Gettysburg Review;* the *Georgia Review; Harvard Review; Kenyon Review; Massachusetts Review; Missouri Review; Narrative; Painted Bride Quarterly; Pleiades; Ploughshares; Poetry Daily; Poetry Northwest; Sewanee Review;* and *Southern Review.*

Particular thanks to the *Massachusetts Review* for the honor of their Anne Halley Prize, and for an atmosphere of welcome as intelligent as their journal.

Thanks to *Best American Poetry 2016* for including "Grief," to the *Pushcart Prize XLII* for including "Spiritual Evaluation," and to *Best American Poetry 2017* for including "Where to Put It." Gratitude to Maya Pindyck and Ruth Vinz for using "Orphan Letter" in *A Poetry Pedagogy for Teachers: Reorienting Classroom Literacy Practices* (2022). Thanks to Tracy K. Smith for featuring "Mebble" on "The Slowdown," and to *Poetry Daily* for featuring "The Boy with the Bolt."

I am honored by Denise Brown, Sara Graef, and Andrew Hsu for so thoughtfully incorporating poems from this book into musical compositions.

Ongoing thanks to: Michael Broek, my MacDowell gift; Jason Koo, for his leo's largeness and loyalty; Michael Loughran, my blue balloon; Kate O'Neill, who placed rocks across the river; Lesley Dormen, who steers me driftingly clear; Constance Merritt, angel of philtrums and sponsor for always; Catie Rosemurgy, for her grave humor; Sarah Stickney, for Solon, Spinoza, cicadas, and so much of this book; Robert Whitehead for his grace; And Eleanor Wilner, for the generosity of her brilliance.

Zack Lesser and Rafa Lesser-Silverman: You are my ways to say luck.

notes

The epigraph from Mahmoud Darwish comes from his "Four Personal Addresses," translated by Munir Akash and Carolyn Forché.

"Ways to Say Luck": In the fourth stanza, the symbol of "how the soul dwells inside space" comes from "Seele Im Raum" by Randall Jarrell.

The tenth stanza refers to Selene, the Greek goddess of the moon. In love with mortal Endymion, Selene offers Endymion anything he wants, and Endymion chooses to sleep forever as her beloved.

"And They Lived": Some details come from Plutarch's *Life of Solon,* translated by Bernadotte Perrin.

"Whatever You Can": The Jewish Museum's installation of metal faces is called "Shalekhet" ("Fallen Leaves," in Hebrew) by Israeli sculptor Menashe Kadishman.

"Die Welt": The "stones of different sizes" form part of the Memorial to Murdered Jews of Europe, designed by architect Peter Eisenman and located in central Berlin.

The words "In exile you leave the perfect order of Berlin" and "When you leave Berlin, you enter the perfect order" come from architect Daniel Libeskind's Garden of Exile in the Jewish Museum of Berlin.

"Tiresias Too": In Ovid's *Metamorphoses,* the shepherd Tiresias is changed into a woman when he disturbs two copulating snakes, then changed again into a man when he sees the snakes seven years later. Because of Tiresias's unique perspective, Hera and Zeus ask him if men or women can experience more pleasure, and he confirms Zeus's claim that women are more capable of pleasure. To punish him for siding with Zeus, Hera blinds Tiresias. Zeus mitigates this punishment by giving him the power to see the future.

The seventeenth-century philosopher Baruch Spinoza's theory on the nature of prophets comes from chapter two of his *Theological-Political Treatise.* Translation by Samuel Shirley.

"A Section from the Myth about Psyche and Cupid" refers to the 2012 New Delhi rape and murder of medical student Jyoti Singh. One of six men who raped, tortured, and threw Jyoti Singh from a moving bus was seventeen-year-old Raju Afroz. Sentenced as a juvenile to three years of rehabilitation, Raju Afroz was released in 2015.

The defense lawyer quoted in the poem is M. L. Sharma. More information can be found in the documentary "India's Daughter," which has been banned in India.

"Dome of the Rock, Rock of the Tunnel": A 2016 video shows Police Officer Kevin Ferguson drag a thirteen-year-old boy across several yards in Anaheim, California, and then fire a gun near the boy's head. Officer Kevin Ferguson was not reprimanded. The boy was arrested. Twenty-three of the three hundred people who protested were also arrested.

The poet whose body has never been found is Federico García Lorca, conflated here with the contemporary poet Cynthia Dewi Oka who began a 2017 poetry reading with the words, "I am here because I am scared." The line "Those who migrate are inventors" belongs to Cynthia Dewi Oka.

"Take It Everything:" The citations of Galileo come from notes he wrote in his copy of a book by Cardinal Johannes Baptista Morino. Galileo's notes were attached to the back of the book: "To prove his power, God could have made birds with gold bones and silver veins, with tiny wings and eyes heavier than lead . . . but he wanted to show his pleasure in simplicity, in ease."

Tommaso Campanella was a Dominican monk imprisoned beneath the Castle of Naples for twenty-seven years during the Spanish Inquisition.

"Poem about Chuck E. Cheese a Friend Posted on Facebook" cites Campbell McGrath's "Benediction for the Savior of Orlando."

For nine hundred years, the Ben Ezra Synagogue in Cairo kept letters, decrees, poems, and lists in a hidden storage space ("genizah" in Hebrew) that scholars discovered in 1896. This material illuminates countless aspects of previously unimagined history.

George Zimmerman shot Trayvon Martin to death on February 26, 2012, while Martin was walking to a store to buy Skittles. Zimmerman was acquitted by claiming self-defense through Florida's "Stand Your Ground" law. Trayvon Martin was not armed.

The "hero / for democracy" refers to the journalist Daniel Pearl, killed in 2002.

The painter in "The Delta" is Carlos Páez Vilaró. His son was one of sixteen survivors of the 1972 Uruguayan Air Force plane crash, trapped for two months under an avalanche in the Andes Mountains.

"Philtrum": The story of the angel who shaped the hollow above the upper lip was written as midrash, or early commentary on the Torah.